EXTREME DINOSAURS

WORLD's SCARIEST DINOSAURS

Rupert Matthews

www.raintreepublishers.co.uk
Visit our website to find out
more information about
Raintree books.

To order:
☎ Phone 0845 6044371
▤ Fax +44 (0) 1865 312263
✉ Email myorders@raintreepublishers.co.uk

Customers from outside the UK please telephone +44 1865 312262

Raintree is an imprint of **Capstone Global Library Limited**,
a company incorporated in England and Wales having its
registered office at 7 Pilgrim Street, London, EC4V 6LB –
Registered company number: 6695582

Text © Capstone Global Library Limited 2012
First published in hardback in 2012
The moral rights of the proprietor have been asserted.

Edited by Rebecca Rissman and Laura Knowles
Designed by Richard Parker
Picture research by Mica Brancic
Originated by Capstone Global Library Ltd
Printed and bound in China by CTPS

ISBN 978 1 406 23464 0
15 14 13 12 11
10 9 8 7 6 5 4 3 2 1

British Library Cataloguing in Publication Data
Matthews, Rupert.
World's scariest dinosaurs. -- (Extreme dinosaurs)
567.9-dc22
A full catalogue record for this book is available from
the British Library.

Acknowledgements
We would like to thank the following for permission to
reproduce images: © Capstone Publishers pp. **4** (James Field),
5 (James Field), **6** (James Field), **7** (Steve Weston), **8** (James
Field), **9** (James Field), **10** (Steve Weston), **11** (Steve Weston),
12 (Steve Weston), **13** (James Field), **14** (James Field), **15**
(Steve Weston), **16** (James Field), **17** (James Field), **18** (James
Field), **19** (James Field), **20** (James Field), **21** (James Field), **23**
(Steve Weston), **25** (Steve Weston); © Miles Kelly Publishing
pp. **24** (Fiametta Dogi), **27** (Mike Saunders);
iStockphoto p. **29** (© Arpad Benedek).

Background design features reproduced with permission of
Shutterstock/© Szefei/© Fedorov Oleksiy/© Oleg Golovnev/
© Nuttakit.

Cover image of a *Tyrannosaurus* reproduced with permission
of © Capstone Publishers/James Field.

We would like to thank Nathan Smith for his invaluable help
in the preparation of this book.

Every effort has been made to contact copyright holders of
material reproduced in this book. Any omissions will be
rectified in subsequent printings if notice is given to the
publishers.

Contents

Some words are shown in bold, **like this**.
You can find out what they mean by
looking in the glossary.

A scary world

The world was a terrifying place 100 million years ago. **Dinosaurs** far larger than any animal alive today walked the land. Some of them were fierce hunters, while others were scary beasts with horns and spikes.

The tyrant king

Tyrannosaurus was a huge meat-eater that lived in North America. It could open its strong jaws very wide, ready to plunge its teeth into **prey**. *Tyrannosaurus* did not only hunt for food. It used its sense of smell to find dead, rotting bodies that it could feast on.

Tyrannosaurus

Did you know?

Tyrannosaurus had sharp teeth over 25 centimetres long. That's longer than your lower arm!

Fatty terror

Spinosaurus may have been the most massive hunting **dinosaur** of them all. It weighed about 18 tonnes. That is the same as four Asian elephants! *Spinosaurus* probably hunted large fish in rivers or swamps. The hump on its back may have been made of fat, similar to a camel's hump. This fat would have been used when food was hard to find.

Did you know?
Some scientists think *Spinosaurus* may also have hunted other dinosaurs.

Clawed killer

Deinonychus was a lethal killing machine. It hunted in groups known as packs. This meant it could kill and eat animals much larger than itself. *Deinonychus* could run at about 48 kilometres an hour when hunting – that is as fast as a race horse!

Did you know?
Deinonychus had a curved claw on its back leg that was nearly 13 centimetres long. It probably used this to slash at victims.

Deinonychus

Handy hunter

The meat-eater *Acrocanthosaurus* measured almost 9 metres. That is as long as two cars. It caught **prey** using its front legs. These were very strong. The clawed fingers could bend forwards or backwards easily.

Did you know?

Acrocanthosaurus probably grabbed a victim with its clawed arms so tightly that it could not escape. The prey was then bitten to death and gobbled up.

Spiked lizard

Styracosaurus had so many spikes on its head that it was given a name that means "spiked lizard". The spikes grew from the back of its skull and were very sharp. Perhaps they were weapons to fight off hunters. This **dinosaur** was about 5.5 metres long, which is three times longer than a motorbike.

Did you know?
Styracosaurus may have lowered its head and waggled the spikes at **rivals** to scare them away.

Mystery killer

Baryonyx was 8.5 metres long, which is as long as five sofas pushed end to end. It is a mystery how it found its food. Some scientists think it used its long, sharp claws to kill other **dinosaurs** for food. Others believe it used its small, sharp teeth to catch fish in rivers. Nobody really knows.

Did you know?

Scientists called the animal *Baryonyx walkeri* after William Walker, who found the **fossils** when out for a walk.

Crested hunter

Dilophosaurus was a hunter that had two crests on its head. Its teeth pointed backwards and its jaw had a kink in it. These may have helped *Dilophosaurus* catch small **prey** such as fish. The first *Dilophosaurus* **fossil** to be found had no crest so the scientist who discovered it left it off his drawing of the **dinosaur**.

Did you know?

In the film **Jurassic** Park, *Dilophosaurus* is shown with a neck frill. No such frill existed.

19

Tyrant ancestor

The hunting **dinosaur** *Guanlong* lived in China. It was about 3 metres long. It could run quickly, leaping to pounce on **prey** and tear them to pieces. It may have lived on the shores of lakes and on riverbanks. It is thought that *Guanlong* was related to *Tyrannosaurus*.

Guanlong

Twilight hunter

Twilight was no time to relax. The hunter *Stenonychosaurus* had very large eyes so it could see well at night. It would **stalk** and kill when others were sleeping.

Stenonychosaurus may have had feathers on its head and arms. These were probably brightly coloured and were held upright to startle other dinosaurs.

feathers

23

Thick heads

One group of plant-eating **dinosaurs** had very thick skulls made of almost solid bone. They are known as Pachycephalosaurs, which means "thick-headed lizards". *Wannanosaurus* was one of the earliest of these dinosaurs. It was less than one metre long. *Pachycephalosaurus* was the biggest. It was as long as an estate car. Perhaps the dinosaurs butted each other in fights.

Wannanosaurus

Pachycephalosaurus

bony skull

Did you know?
The skull of *Pachycephalosaurus* was over 20 centimetres thick.

Elasmosaurus

Dinosaurs were not the only giant creatures to live during the **Mesozoic Era**. In the sea lived gigantic **reptiles**. Turtles grew to be over 4 metres across – as big as a large garden paddling pool. Ichthyosaurs were reptiles that looked and behaved like dolphins. Plesiosaurs were reptiles with large bodies and long necks.

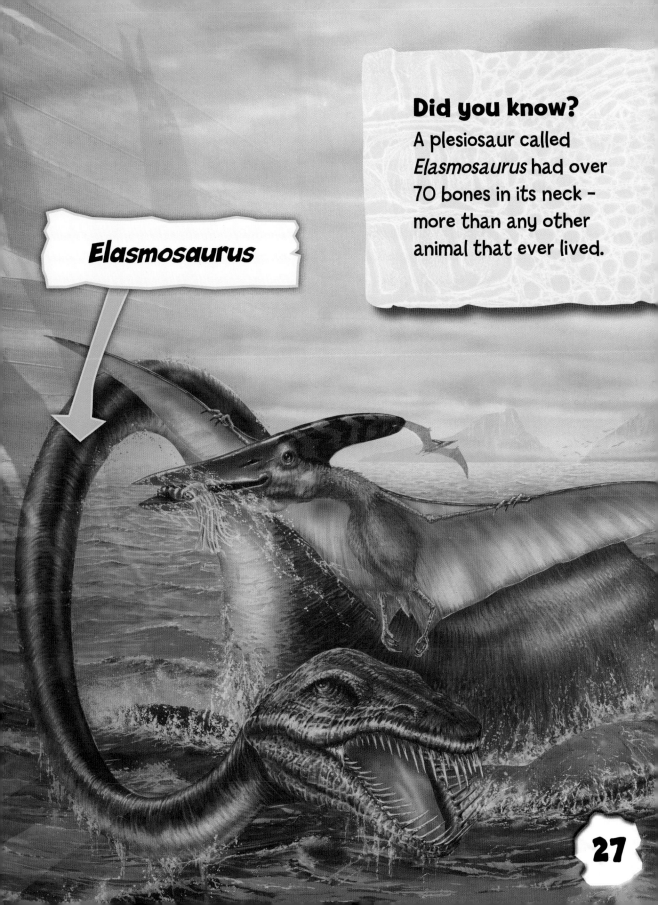

Elasmosaurus

Did you know?

A plesiosaur called *Elasmosaurus* had over 70 bones in its neck – more than any other animal that ever lived.

27

How to become a palaeontologist

Scientists who study **dinosaurs** and other **ancient** animals are called palaeontologists. After finishing school, students study at university to learn how to become a palaeontologist. They learn how to find **fossils** and how to study them. Palaeontologists need to know about the many different sorts of ancient life. It is possible to be a part-time palaeontologist. Some people look for fossils as a hobby at weekends and on holidays.

Glossary

ancient describes something that lived a very long time ago

dinosaur group of animals that lived on land millions of years ago during the Mesozoic Era

fossil part of a plant or animal that has been buried in rocks for millions of years

Jurassic part of Earth's history that began about 200 million years ago and ended about 145 million years ago

Mesozoic Era part of Earth's history that is sometimes called the "Age of Dinosaurs". It is divided into three periods: Triassic, Jurassic, and Cretaceous.

prey animal that is killed by another for food

reptiles cold-blooded animals such as lizards or crocodiles

rival dinosaur competing with another for something such as food

stalk follow quietly and carefully so as not to be heard or seen

twilight time in the evening when the Sun is setting but it is not yet dark

Find out more

Books

Dinosaur Encyclopedia, Caroline Bingham
    (Dorling Kindersley, 2009)
Dinosaurs, Stephanie Turnbull (Usborne, 2006)
Explorers Dinosaurs, Dougal Dixon (Kingfisher, 2010)
First Encyclopedia of Dinosaurs and Prehistoric Life,
    Sam Taplin (Usborne, 2011)

Websites

www.dinosaurden.co.uk
Information about dinosaurs, as well as puzzles and games
can be found on this site.

www.enchantedlearning.com/subjects/dinosaurs
The dinosaur section of this website includes information on
many dinosaurs and fossils.

www.nhm.ac.uk/kids-only/dinosaurs
The Natural History Museum's website has lots of information
about dinosaurs, including facts, quizzes, and games.

www.thedinosaurmuseum.com/html/dinosaur-facts.html
Find out more about dinosaurs on the Dinosaur Museum website.

Index